No Apologies Necessary

Ashley Gooden

BookLeaf
Publishing

India | USA | UK

Presentation by *BookLeaf Publishing*

Web: www.bookleafpub.com

E-mail: info@bookleafpub.com

ISBN: 9789360943400

First edition 2024

PREFACE

In the realm of words, where emotions dance freely and thoughts intertwine, there exists a sanctuary—a space where truth reigns supreme, where vulnerability is celebrated, and where apologies find no home. Welcome to "No Apologies Necessary," a collection of verses that dares to embrace the raw beauty of human experience without reservation.

Within these pages lie echoes of laughter, tears stained with the ink of introspection, and whispers of the soul's deepest yearnings. Each poem is a testament to the power of language to transcend barriers, to bridge divides, and to connect us in our shared humanity.

As you journey through these lines, may you find solace in the resonance of shared experiences, courage in the face of adversity, and inspiration to embrace the full spectrum of your being. For in this space, there is no judgment, no pretense—only the unfiltered expression of what it means to be human.

So, dear reader, I invite you to journey with me into the heart of vulnerability, where apologies are unnecessary, and authenticity reigns supreme. Let these words be a reminder that you are not alone, that your story matters, and that there is beauty in every moment, no matter how fleeting.

Fitting Room Fight

My body and I made a truce in the fitting room
today.
It will be the clothes as the problem and not her.
She committed no crime being this fine.
I pinky promised to choose my true size and not
the lies I fantasized about 3 years ago.
That I will not demand her shrink in this space
to fit the standards that accost her being from
magazine stands and TV screens.
We will not reach a stalemate at outfit 3 and cry
bitter tears over tattered threads that weren't
worth me in the first place.
These outfits will not be bullets I'm already holy.
Even if the putback pile plays mountain at me.
They will go back on the rack and will no longer
weigh, on me giving a damn about my weight.
That is between the scale and gravity.
These clothes will not be a disguise, there will
be no hiding behind random stripes and floral
prints.
We will be sexy, sensible, sassy, classy not
limited and lacking tastiness, and if all else fails
and we're looking for a little less ball gown and
a little more dress down

I tell her we can meet in the middle and land at
comfortable.
My belly can bulge the way she chooses and I
will ornament it nicely.
The shapewear will not suffocate the natural tide
of my chest.
The breaths will not cease while I button up and
if it rubs me the wrong way it will go hang there
disappointed that I refuse to contort for it.
Refuse to suffer discomfort for it.
There is no more war in my wardrobe.
The cavalry against my cellulite will ceasefire.
It will not simply be a draw in the dressing
room.
I will win and my body worn as a trophy.
She comes with me as is at any given moment in
her grace, her size in its entirety, its fullness.
 I won't care if it fits me, she fits me.
 From cell to cell she doesn't have to sell me on
her brilliance anymore.
She gets me from point A to B and to all my
in-between I love you.

Nails

Don't bother me bitch I'm busy making nails I'm too callous from creating keratin to deal with anything negative you say.
For your information, I am constructing something hard to scratch with.
To get that itch to snatch the bitch who thinks I have the time for the bull shit. Your opinion is insignificant.
I'm making me.
Picking up where my mama left off and if I'm going to make something as tough as nails damn sure I'm making quality.
It's something like magic extending from the tip of my fingers.
They pull... they attract.. they cling and crack.
Not as flexible as the back you try to walk on. Store your knives in.
Believe it or not, I have lives in these hands, my fingers they grip but I have to learn to clip away the excess the unnecessary lest I stretch too thin too fragile, and become vulnerable breakable under stress.
Unable to sift through the mess your mess, my mess.

The message is simple I'd rather build myself
from the ground up now.
 And it gets me wound up how I lived any other
way.
On any given day I served so many other
masters constructing palaces, castles tall, and
cathedrals with beautiful blood-stained glass
walls.
Now I'm holding hammers, no I'm throwing
hammers doing my damage. Till all I can
manage to do is sit here with my new foundation
just me and these Nails.

I write Poetry

I used to doubt that what I write is poetry.
How could something this amazing find itself in
my books?
Evolving from my experiences into words with
deeper meanings.
Do I have a license to wield this pen to scribble
nouns and verbs to reverberate movements?
Express pain and even one day leave the dragon
slain solely because I don't know where to buy a
sword.
But damn girl I can rhyme some words good,
gooder goodly make the ungodly sing a sweet
testimony.
Own my art my craft and place it in my alabaster
box lain at his feet.
Marry my similes to my homophones.
No homophobia please because my words are
bipartisan and can part seas if I tell them to.
Be the glue to mend wounds and see those of
different hues hold hands openly. My words
open springs and quench the nations thirsty for
change.
What it take to get all this power?
The power to make the impossible possible,
make emotions life-like.

Make the stagnant animate and the people
aggregate.
I think it takes a steady handle on reality and the
ability to release it and create your own.
Like a greased-up pig you don't want to contain
it and it can't be controlled.
If the truth is told you no longer have to hold on
to pain.
The pain took the truth away simply and made
me forget that.
I've been validated and venerated by better souls
than me.
It's reminds me
I am spoken word in the third person, with
poetry written in the acidic base of my anatomy.
The native language that grew foreign to me
until I opened my mouth to speak volumes and
let my mind be consumed with beauty.

C- Minus

Nothing irks me more than a c- minus
individual.
To watch and be a bystander to such mediocrity
is a betrayal to my archetype. My A type.
I have carried the C- and they just barely pass
me in line for the resources in this market.
I am tired of holding the A note when the middle
C takes the credit.
They take and they get round and content while I
stand tall and thin waiting for someone to
acknowledge All that C minus energy taking up
so much room.
My seat at the table.
Needless to say, I will raise a C minus baby. And
they will conquer and reap the benefits with as
little effort as humanely possible.
I will not raise another A-plus personality.
Baby I know you will have the A in potential.
But I'm left as the A in exhausted.
C yourself to the front of every line without
breaking a sweat. Show them you can be
anything effortlessly.
I will continue to hate the C- because I was
raised to put the A in slave and I refuse that
carry on that Legacy.

You will not Acrobat your way around their
desires the way I was taught.
 Live in your Contentment and create.

Savior

Who saves them?
The ones that didn't ask to be born into poverty.
The ones who never had passages from
Deuteronomy read to them.
 How far does his mercy extend in this plain of
reality?
Not speaking smartly just out of pure innocence
and curiosity.
I am afraid of my mortality and I can't seem to
hold onto hope as tightly.
Who saves me the bitter and depressed from the
repressed rage that lives inside of me?
My parents have all but abandoned me I have a
home physically but mentally spiritually
emotionally straw houses are my domicile and
the pack has me on their scent map.
I try humility and subservience.
Underdog is my middle first and last name.
Not looking for a savior just empathy.
Who saves those with alternative sexuality and
an unrecognizable in their own mirror identity?
Where does grace leave me and adorn those
more "righteous and holy"?
No map to guide me because the scrolls left are
riddled in controversy.

Help me.
Although it's not heard audibly these screams are
absorbed passively in my capillaries.
They reside in the oxygen that fuels me.
And as a woman, the grace in me extends like
roots from trees grounded in the concrete.
In need a we a sort of uh self-made family.
I need a God who believes in me as much as I in
him.
No grim reaping.
What I sow is no discontent but a need for my
own wisdom with ignorance weeded from my
vocabulary.
Again I say help me.

Celebrate

Baby, I woke up looked in the mirror and all I
wanna do is celebrate.

I see the hate comments published on my skin in
permanent ink and I'm going to love them away
like they're past expiration dates on imperishable
goodness

Hatred marred my steps to this point but now all
I have are dancing feet. chains left imprints of
broken spirits and that ancestry revealed to me
my roots are deeper than the mines planted to
destroy me.
This is story telling pigment.
Passed down more than pain it granted presence.
It makes me glow brighter.
Contrary to the association of dark and the
nighttime I only bring sunshine.

I'm not puttin on no clothes.
Look at this fight.
These scars were specially embroidered and
they're thick like me.
They show reverence to the inside and out brawl
I took on to love all of me.

My best my worst my everything.
You can't touch me today.
Desire me admire me from afar.
Too often it's happened without permission.
Taken for granted.
Taken advantage of.
Don't get me started.... This majesty is above
me.
It graced me.
They want to taste this sun-kissed chocolate as it
drapes me.
God himself trusted me to wear it.
Dark down to the bones.
The color of my soul.
This sweet nectar existence.
Needs a love that isn't hesitant its as bold as my
hue.
It's as personal as healing this joy I can't help but
to feel.
Ego doesn't suit me and vanity don't fit.
Conditioned to fear dark and now I can only
embrace it.
In this dark where my eyes are wide open.
Skin scarred and holy.
So yea I'm gonna dance away the hurt till it
hurts.
Only while I'm celebrating me.

Ruminate

Certain animals need to eat their food "twice" to
absorb all the nutrients.
They regurgitate, and ruminate when they can't
fully assimilate what they've consumed
Can't seem to assimilate
 That seems to be my relationship with my
mistakes lately.
I need to make them over again and again before
I absorb the lesson.
Need to dip my eyes in the warning signs more
than once to soak in the message.
 Didn't work for my hands either because the
more I touched you the more about you I wanted
to understand.
Gotta give my mind a second go around before it
can all come through.
But fuck that all I want is a second go around to
get to know you.
Something about second chances when I
should've gotten it right the first time hurt more
than Mama's lashes when I should've heard it
when she said the first time.
You don't learn you feel.
I can't bridge the gap.
Difficult to accept the defect the deficit.

Take it in before you defecate defeated praying
to pass it one more good time. Don't want
fingers too short gut let the opportunities slip
through my hands too slick to grasp the gravity
that I may only have so long on this Earth.
I don't want to ruminate, remain in the same
space.
Until all I get is the mere reflection, the echo.
My grandma taught me to sew once upon a time.
Fixed her weathered hands to bring me a little
sunshine and I just couldn't get it the first time.
My clumsy fingers fumbling needle and thread
not knowing it was the last time she could teach
me anything but how to die gracefully.
I don't blame that baby for messing up or even
giving up but now this woman realizes the
importance of catching a moment holding it
precious squeeze out every ounce of joy juice,
meaty memory absorb all you can in every little
infinity you can find.
Sometimes a replay is just as good as the first
impression and sometimes you will find yourself
fixated on a first time fleeting too far to be fully
immersed, captured, digested, and assimilated.

A Woman's Revolution

Truth be told I've had wrath withheld, and more
than gold I want it that burdens my soul to begin
to unfold.
I want blood of all shades drawn with the
sharpest blade from wrists balled into fists
because they refuse to release their peace of
mind.
The lost dreams of sleepless nights.
Tears of the women who left the earth without
knowing an inkling of their full worth.
The sweat of women who built themselves to
crowned heads from shackled ankles.
This would make the fuel for a spirit fire ignited
in the core of someone who always chose to love
more.
With this flame, I'm choosing to fight without
gloves knowing I've lived without love for
myself and that hurt more than bloody knuckles
on concrete harder than the skulls of
hard-headed niggas who can't say they've
reached the end of the rainbow.
They don't know what treasure looks like, how it
tastes, and the sounds it makes when it's satisfied

Are you even men yet cursing the very oasis you
emerged from spitting on its beauty calling it
cowardly synonyms like pussy.
It's no misnomer because what I learned is that
they are merciless and from bones tear the skin
of their prey before their prey can pray for
judgment day.
I'm livid at those living with the interpretation
that "I am less" because God chose to bless me
with one and topped it off with skin darker so
the scars you inflict can fade into silk.
Somehow they are misunderstood for novelty
that you find when feeling thrifty and wouldn't it
be nifty to take the rare jewel that wears my
body gracefully? Pretend you didn't find me on a
throne and maybe next time I'll know to leave
the jester alone.

Rest

We stop we stay we rot we lay down in our own
filth.
When there is better there is always better.
And God damn it I'm an opportunity getter.
Not a time waster might as well paster that on
my forehead that I want to get ahead by any
means at night I screams to escape the small and
mediocre.
Tired of the Awkward the mistake.
Hearing that I walked away from the poker
game too early.
I didn't know when to hold watch as I fold over
and under.
Never more do I want to wonder the shoulda,
coulda, who would I be.
If I was truly me, and the cost of staying alive
was truly free and not a fantasy.
I don't have excuses just pain and scars that I
plan to run from, work through, dues to pay
dragons to slay, and when it's all said and done
beds to lay in.
Not rot, not degrade, decay, delay.
I will not wilt away if I take a step away to
 BREATHE, BREATHE, BREATHE.

I do not have to grieve who I once was, the hard
worker, overthinker binge drinker.
I'm not deceased, my bed is not a grave with the
TV keeping vigil and a bouquet of potato chips
embalmed in sweat, regret and a sheen of
embarrassment.
 It's just all rest.

Rebellion

We need a rebellion.
Like a fuck you to the status quo.
The woe of the creatives the antagonist to the
catalyst of movements.
Let us be renegades of the revolution.
Respectability can see me in the back for
disregarding black bodies black hair, but
attempts to colonize black flair.
This is a warning to the implementors,
dementors sucking the soul from society. I'm
sorry your grandma wasn't on her knees at the
alter call.
That she didn't hold you in her arms while you
bawled after momma discipline came down a
little to hard.
You clearly weren't woken up on Saturday
morning too gospel music learning how fi clean
ya own yard
 That there be making us, whatever don't be
breaking us, or taking us.
They Just keep shaking us like a can of pop till
we explode in an angsty rage. Just wanna
Breaking free from systemic cages.
 How should we behave if we really want
change?

What emotions should I express when I'm
getting less than?
I can't just take it on my, back, knees.
I'm On my feet when I'm othered.
Mouth big, heart full Ten toes tethered on solid
ground
When They be Letting the expected penetrate
the spaces.
Discrimination against the faces.
Tired of pacing back and forth in a panic..
I gotta make that emotion useful.
It will be less than graceful and you're gonna
hear a mouthful.
But I'm gonna be grateful when my grandbabies
have full bellies eyes full of bright-ass
opportunities.
 Hands full and unscarred from the lashes of
oppression.
Nana did all of the heavy lifting.
Sip on some easy living.
Now that the powers that been be gone.
Get me a black picket fence for my pretty ass
lawn and all seats for my table sitting 10 feet
long.
Let's sit where rebellion turns into revelations.
Sit in the better world of our creation.
Part out own red seas to promised lands and
We better not let it take no 40 years neither.

Crypt of Broken Dreams

Dug a grave with my failures and he jumped in.
Ready to die.
Not for me but with me, which is not the
sacrifice you think it is.
He thought we would take a gondola down the
Styx and hold hands in Hades. He wanted to
make death a team sport.
A bonding experience between two copulating
corpses.
So we kept digging to find our peace in the sick
pestilence that is dying slowly. We knew it was
wrong smelled wrong but love has no senses.
I had to realize love had no sense and would not
bring sense to senseless and I'm so glad it wasn't
scentless because then salvation would not have
found me. I would not have been dragged out by
this ragged body.
I had to hide my nakedness in lies about sanity
while the cracks in my skin and my smile kept
widening.
Broadening the scars keloid calloused candy
cane stripes lined my very being.
It was ugly to see because even majesty could be
musty, dusty but baby cleaned up I'm a sight to
see.
Cliche to say it was truth that set me free from
the Crypt of broken dreams.

Infinity

The concept of infinity is something we know
intrinsically.
Not me physically but how we define divinity.
It goes on continuously.
No end in sight but it might apply both
microscopic and universally.
Number of grains of sand on a beach to the
number of 9s after the point when you divide 3
by 3.
From the school to the church house infinity
makes its own rules makes its ownself known.
Omnipresent both felt and shown.
How I describe my soul compared to a whole
universe. It can't be captured, bought, sold,
taught or told.
As I grow old she grows out of time both forever
and never at the same damn time.
Can't measure it tame it, contain it.
But I can live and breathe it believe in it.
Believe that I can live infinitely not in time but
in consistency impacting the people around me.
Infinite in the way I lead.
Infinite till the day I breathe out and my impact
is infinite intact in fact so infinite my enemies
will mourn me and my influence surpasses the
year 3 thousand. Never ending not just blending
but mending extending to infinity.

What do we kiss for

It's become routine regimented contact
Do we kiss over shared interest, a sense of pride
Lips no lo longer seamlessly gliding over the
other in passion but practice
I'd never kiss over malice but I hate the
structured sentiments
We kiss in greeting, over the simplicity of
meeting a need.
We weed out the emotion and no longer kiss
over all-nighters in each other's arms.
It's always a simple peck or when the pecker in
your pants becomes erect.
Not simply because the curving of my neck
looked inviting and you were overcome with
regret over not doing it sooner.
I used to kiss from head to toe because I couldn't
imagine a reality where the skin of my lips
weren't analogous to your all over.
What do we kiss for?
No formal reason assigned to the meeting of our
most vulnerable opening.
It could've been the certain glisten of your eyes
in the sunlight gravitating my being to yours.
Or the growing cold of coffee awaiting
enthralling conversation.

The contents of your brain leaving me overcome
with emotion.
I can't help but to taste the words as they leave
your larynx I'm famished for you.
Why don't we kiss over core memories,
reality-bending occurrences anymore?
It should punctuate a paradigm shift.
Now it just lifts your manhood and we seem to
perform mouth to mouth till it's dusks and we're
cleaning off each other's musks maintaining
some form of familiarity.
I can't just do this with anybody so why waste
the kisses?
Why spend the limited lip contact on anything
less than what makes happily ever after.
Save them for the rains on Sunday afternoons.
Save them for the morning picnic after no sleep
chatting about family members we wished we
had the chance to meet.
Let those milliseconds mean something.
Like an abbreviated eternity let them be loaded
with love passion, an undying devotion to the
cells the atoms that come closer than others.
From fingernails grazing to hairs raising and
fabric fornicating.
Every point of contact be pure in their intentions
to penetrate my heart, my mind and the oxytocin
combined.

Lock in the microscopic memories a world, a
lifetime fully lived.
Fully realized in an instant.
Find me in a meadow in a field of flowers in the
rain and Plant one where the sun shines

That One Ex

There's still parts of you in me that I'll never get
rid of.
It's like looking in the mirror turns into ripped
polaroids of who we were together.
Don't think I'll ever manage to manage the
mannerisms of yours I've maintained. So I'll
water them let them grow eb and flow in and out
of me daily.
I see You are a part of me I even wrinkle my
nose the way you used to.
Can't help that I've absorbed the parts of you I've
wanted to keep in the lining of my way to small
jeans shorts.
Make no mistake I've purged the poison you
forced down my throat in drink me bottles
decorated with frills of affection.
My liver still aches a colander for the filth I fed
upon by your hand.
They were choices a bitter me can't explain
away.
I was never forced to stay
The trauma nailed my feet to the ground as the
house fell down around us. Sifting through the
rubble I found broken glass and fractured wood.

Salt and pepper shakers I bought to make us
palatable.
The knife set, you know the ones where we
made sheaths of each other's hearts to store
them.
I found wreckage and damage, damning
evidence we were no good for one another.
But I also found they way you laughed when
you told me my nose was too big. The way you
danced forget your dad.
The way you crossed your arms when you were
cross with me.
The creasing of your forehead when you
forfeited the fight because I'm the one that's
right.
They followed me to a new home and I display
them like tchotchkes.
Little quirks on me, new people fell in love with.
Yea, I used parts of your personality to pick up
chicks but only because I know they once
worked on me..

Cemetery Flowers

The smell of fresh cemetery flowers on my
walk.
I sense the shift in energy as my yellow crocks
hit green pathway.
I look around at the multicolor ornamenting the
marble.
Bodies just below the fallen petals like they die a
little faster when commissioned to echo their
surroundings
Decaying carnations drew me in and gave me a
message of impermanence in the most beautiful
package
 It may not be here but there will be a space in
the universe holding space for who I once was..
and it hastens my steps.
 I am not afraid of being in the past tense for I
was once future and so were the flowers and the
identities that now lay underneath these trees.
I always wonder why flowers are lain at grave
sites and burial grounds.
Ashes to ashes dust to dust then flowers then
people.
After all like flowers we showed our best self
with one foot in the grave

Instead of laying flowers on my final resting place.
 Instead of the flowers resting with me let me rest among the flowers.
Pour what's left of me into a flower bed. Let me tend to the roses one last time. Let my dying act bring life.
The sting of death lies beneath the scent of daffodils in this place.
Not pungent by any means but present in all the corners like traced outlines.
I couldn't stay too long because the smell of flowers and death are becoming indistinguishable.
And they burn my eyes.
I couldn't be crying there is no one for me here.
Then I guess I'm mourning this morning I will never have again adoring the flowers of the cemetery.

Pussy

I named my Pussy, Wisdom, Mercedes, Alexis, Aston Martin, Chanel, Tesla, Gucci, Louie, Balmain, Luther, Little, el-Shabazz, Ghandi, Parks, Tubman, Shakur, Wallace, Knowles, Carter, Armani, Fenty, Taj Mahal worthy, Eiffel Tower high, Jet blue sky, , First Class seat mile high club, Paint me pretty, The blessed, the whole, the great. The Remembered, honoured, revered, respected and protected, salvation, holy, holey, lil grippy, grip me, hold me, And if you can't remember all that I'm sure she'll settle for the super soaker 5000.

Disasters

I wrote you a poem last year and in that time I
learned it takes more than words. Patience faith
and shaky hands unafraid to reach out for yours.
Unsure feet eager to jump into the deep dark
scary end of life with me.
Mouths unafraid to speak tornados into the small
rooms we shared followed by staring into the
dark corners wondering if this should continue.
It requires a kind of Courage conviction with
strict boundaries that can still do gymnastics
enough to flex and bend for one another.
Baby it takes more than love to live through
what we do.
When the wildfires in your eyes burn brighter
than the hope for our future don't be afraid to cry
and let the rainbows inside because I promise
like God did to refuse to let the flood rise and
drown the saplings we planted in our love bed.
We seem to both inflict pain but let the passion
and pleasure override the bitter battered bruises
that populate under the soft spots of our eyes.
We rub the tears that tsunami after foot stomp
earthquakes and whirlwinds of yells when
soft-spoken words aren't sufficient enough to
love you the way anger thinks I should.

I don't want to erupt and destroy our Pompeii
while I'm still paying collateral for the past
disasters.
Baby we are the aftermath to the aftermath of
events that destroy lives.
We are the reconstruction, the road to
resurrection from the shambles and ashes of
former souls.
We are the refuge for one another the safety
blanket to smother out past flames.
I really hope you feel the same when I say I love
you past, through, and after disasters.

Fields

I want to belong in my own home.
The land that's not mine originally. where I have
to adapt but not like it was given to me.
Back then they had to take the freedom
forcefully.
Decades later we still fight to remain free.
I seem to stand in land both foreign and familiar.
Land of freedoms bittersweet when one lives in
this color.
Land built on the back of ancestors 10 times
over bent over in the pain of underserved
cruelties.
Today it seems to be the same but with domestic
enemies.
I sang for freedom.
Francis Scott held the key to shackles and his
melody is meant to represent me. They sang to
cripple and keep down.
Well, we have the keys to our own movement
now.
For centuries we were on our knees in agony and
today I bend because my very existence is
defiance and I defy the odds set against me
fearlessly.
I kneel for those fallen in the fields.

Not just the playing but America the battlefield
filled with those unarmed and killed.
Shed red under a blue sky at the mercy of white
hands.
Why the hell should I have to stand and cover a
broken heart with my tired of praying so hard for
the safety of my people right hand.
Go ask the unmarked grave of a black man, Who
gave me the peaceful rebellion I was promised?

Holy

The moment between the silence and the first
note.
When you're about to shout the first sound.
The face before the force.
The breath before the bars even dropped.
The blink between the introduction and the first
word spoken.
It's inspiring the way you're desiring more the
way you want to pour into your audience.
The art be your Bible read the scripture your
soul authors.
Your message the good news fill the pews on
Sunday morning, Tuesday night. Eyes so bright
as you lay yourself as sacrificial, they don't get
the vision lay it out bleeding for the masses.
Your energy, execution, evolution they take it
consume you exhume the body of your work.
The spirit looms clouds raining saturate the
room get lost in the space turn maze from the
sound waves you create.
We are the creators the universe living through
itself.
We are the beauty bouncing back.
Release the energy and it will be returned
tenfold.
Let the art you create be worth the beholding
just as much as it was worth to create.

Questions

What is the difference between a growing pain
and a pack up your shit and get to-going pain?
How much does a divorce cost?
No silly things can't be equated to frivolous
dollars.
How much of your dignity do you lay at the
judge's feet before he'll cross out the lines till
death do us part?
Why do we make love and a piece of paper
written in removable words synonyms?
You can't write miscarriages as a condition for
this love even though time and time again it has
proven to be one?
Okay, miscarriage is a bit of a stretch but let's
change it to infidelity.
What if this other person kept the air from
seeping out of your lover's dying soul shouldn't
that fall within the boundaries of better or
worse?
When did Bibles say love was conditional?
How could marriage have been considered
unconditional the very creator of love himself
set conditions in which his love is capable of
eternal damnation.

No matter how bad I hurt you I will never be the
first one and you have survived worse than this
in your covenant with Christ.
Love = pain = marriage= promise = praise =
adoration = abomination = risk = reward =
unconditional = conditional = beginning = end =
alpha and omega = God = YOU

Dedication

To every man that hurt me and even to the me that hurt myself I wrote a poem about you and I hope one day you not only get to hear it, but feel the healing that came out of pain and the masterpiece masked behind a mistake

www.ingramcontent.com/pod-product-compliance
Lightning Source LLC
Chambersburg PA
CBHW071232140726